MANUELA B

KT-140-115

Goya

Fundación Amigos del Museo
del Prado

Floor plan of the Prado Museum

SECOND FLOOR

80
83 82 81
79
76 77 78

15 16a 17a
a
14 15 16
16b
28
27
9a 10a
7a 8a 10
8 9 10 11 12
8b 9b 10b 26
25
3 4 5 6 24
1
40 41 42 43 44

51a 51

Upper Goya entrance

Lower Goya entrance

LOWER FLOOR

FIRST FLOOR

Murillo entrance

Velázquez entrance

BASEMENT

Third edition: 2000

Cover and interior design by Ángel Uriarte
Translation by María Luisa Balseiro
Axonometric projections by Ana Pazó Espinosa
Edition by Carmen Ponce de León and Manuel Florentín
Layout by Antonio Martín

© Manuela B. Mena Marqués
© Fundación Amigos del Museo del Prado
  ISBN: 84-95452-01-4
  Depósito legal: M-1560-2000
  Impreso en Varoprinter, S.A. C/ Artesanía, 17. Pol. Ind Coslada (Madrid)
  Printed in Spain

Introduction

The paintings of Francisco de Goya y Lucientes are among the most unique and defining values of the Prado, both in artistic and historical terms, and the sum of his works in all media amounts to a specific museum within the Museum. There are almost 150 pictures by him, and that corpus, combined with the Museum's holdings of more than 500 drawings and the etchings series, renders it possible to study here better than anywhere else one of the greatest personalities in Spanish painting and indeed in world art. Goya's canvases are valuable by themselves; but an additional boon of the Prado collection lies in the chance it affords to view them in the context of Spanish painting, of Velázquez and Murillo, whom Goya profoundly admired, and of the great European artists whose works he had known since youth, such as Titian, Rubens, Tiepolo or Mengs. Goya's approach connects smoothly with the last tendencies of the eighteenth century, so that his early style may be compared to French rococo, or to such a belated sequel of Italian classical baroque as may be found in Corrado Giaquinto, the better to identify what his art owed to tradition and what was truly modern and revolutionary in his conception of painting.

The works which once decorated the walls of the Quinta del Sordo, the so-called 'Black Paintings', close Goya's collection in the Prado, along with the portrait of Muguiro, which may have been the last canvas painted by him. They are among the artistic ensembles that have spawned a more extensive literature, and with them the Prado Museum stands on the threshold of modernity. Frightening, 'black' as to their meaning, dense with the darkest desires of man, their strange and compelling beauty, as far removed from the dainties of rococo refinement as from the icy perfection of the neoclassical rules in which Goya himself had been schooled, places Spanish art among the harbingers of the modern world. By themselves they lay open, better than any written commentary or exposition, the development of a mind that reached into the future, as geniuses typically do.

Chronologically, the rooms devoted to Goya in the Prado start with his sets of tapestry cartoons. Except for some odd pieces preserved in other collections, the Museum owns virtually the whole ensemble of those works, which marked the starting point of his art and the beginning of his activity at court. These big-scale canvases, painted to be used as models by the weavers of the newly-created Fábrica de Tapices de Santa Bárbara, demonstrate Goya's compositional gifts, his sense of colour, the vigour of his pictorial technique and his awareness of the Old Masters and the Antique, as well as his masterly aptitude to apprehend reality in wonderfully fresh ways.

A superb sequence of portraits allows the visitor to the Prado to trace the steps of Goya in this difficult genre, where success required that the painter combine the skill to produce a likeness with a talent for covert flattery, representational inventiveness and, much less easy to define but nonetheless essential, the ability to capture unambiguously the inner individuality of his sitters.

The Prado is fortunate to own two specimens of still life painting by Goya. That genre had attained its highest excellence in the seventeenth century, when the defining features of the Spanish *bodegón* were finally laid down, but it would still find in Goya one of its finest practitioners.

The Goya collection also includes some outstanding pieces in other genres, such as that of history painting, in which the artist narrates a story of some importance, though not always related to actual events; consistent with classical tradition, in Goya that kind of work is always underpinned by his concern with men and their actions. Foremost within this group are the two large canvases dealing with the War of Independence.

The *capricho* or 'fancy piece', a typically eighteenth-century conception, was endowed by Goya with unique qualities of full-fledged modernity and individuality. The Prado houses an exceptionally large and varied array of such works, further enriched by recent acquisitions. An isolated example from the 1793 set presented to the Academy of San Fernando, *Strolling Players*, signals the start of his artistic independence, as he himself emphasized in his letters; but there are others, such as the small *The Duchess of Alba and 'La Beata'*, or *Witches in Flight*, that bear witness to the creative freedom foreshadowed in cartoon sketches like *The Meadow of San Isidro*.

Besides the works already mentioned, any visit to the Prado's Goya collection must of course include the extraordinary *Majas*, one of them naked, the other fully clothed.

The Decoration of the Dining Room of the Crown Prince and Princess in the Palace of El Escorial, 1775

HOUNDS ON A CHAIN (CAT. NO. 753), DECOY HUNTING (CAT. NO. 2856), A HUNTING PARTY (CAT. NO. 2857), A HUNTER LOADING HIS RIFLE (CAT. NO. 5539), A HUNTER WITH HIS HOUNDS (CAT. NO. 805), THE ANGLER (CAT. NO. 5542)

In 1775, while still working under the direction of his brother-in-law Bayeu, Goya secured his first commission as a painter of tapestry cartoons to decorate the Crown prince and princess' dining room in the Escorial Palace. There Goya would strike a new departure from the traditional iconography of great hunts, depicting everyday scenes in a realistic style.

The Decoration of the Dining Room of the Crown Prince and Princess in the Palace of El Pardo, 1776-1778

The palace of El Pardo, set in a magnificent park near Madrid that had been a royal hunting ground from early times, was again put to use by the Bourbon kings as a leisure retreat, especially since the accession of the nature-loving Charles III, and became one of their favourite residences. The decorating of this palace that combined with the enlightened tastes of the time and the desire of monarchs to enter into closer terms with their subjects, may explain the choice of subject matter from daily life and popular amusements: the portrayal of Madrid *majos* and *majas*, or smart young men and women from the lower classes, is an absolute novelty.

THE PICNIC (Cat. No. 768)

A group of *majos* on the bank of the Manzanares River, with the hermitage of the Virgen del Puerto clearly identifiable on the right.

THE DANCE ON THE BANK OF THE MANZANARES RIVER (Cat. No. 769)
The rhythm of the counterposed couples getting ready for the dance makes for a scene of great beauty. The dance shown is the popular *seguidilla*, less lively than the famous *fandango*.

A BRAWL AT THE VENTA NUEVA (Cat. No. 770)

Describing this composition in his invoice, Goya supplied some noteworthy par-

9

ticulars, e. g. the fact that the men gathering at the *venta*, or road inn, are "coachmen and muleteers from several provinces of Spain", recognizable by their garb, such as "the man from Murcia" with his back turned in the foreground. The brawl started over a game of cards, and everyone has more or less violently entered the fray.

A WALK IN ANDALUSIA
(Cat. No. 771)

This is a direct forerunner of some of the most characteristic etchings in the *Caprichos* series, dealing with the intrigues of love and jealousy.

THE PARASOL
(Cat. No. 773)

Here is one of the loveliest examples of Goya's early painting. His acquaintance with the Old Masters is applied unobtrusively.

BOYS BLOWING A BLADDER (Cat. No. 776)
BOYS PICKING FRUIT (Cat. No. 777)

These are among Goya's earliest portrayals of childhood, but they already show his full grasp of the candor and liveliness of children's games.

The Decoration of the Antechamber to the Bedroom of the Crown Prince and Princess in the Palace of El Pardo, 1778

The Decoration of the Bedroom of the Crown Prince and Princess in the Palace of El Pardo, 1778-1779

The Decoration of the Antechamber to the Bedroom of the Crown Prince and Princess in the Palace of El Pardo, 1779-1780

In October 1777, as Goya was completing the cartoons for the dining room of the Crown prince and princess in El Pardo, he was ordered to go on with sets for their sleeping quarters in that palace. Some of the resulting pieces are among the best-known in his oeuvre, e. g. *The Crockery Vendor*, *The Bullfight* or *Boys Playing Soldiers*. The bedroom set focuses on glimpses of Madrid life.

ANTECHAMBER (1778)

THE BLIND GUITARIST
(Cat. No. 778)

detail

Goya described it in minute detail, referring to the fashionable gentleman as "a foreigner" and mentioning the black waterseller and a baker: this is the world of those 'street cries' that were first portrayed by artists in late sixteenth-century Italy.

11

BEDROOM (1778-1779)

THE CROCKERY VENDOR
(Cat. No. 780)

One of the most elaborate compositions in the series, Goya setting the static but emotionally conflicting foreground, with the young girls, the old woman and the vendor, against the swift movement of the coach carrying the lady. As in the best pieces by Watteau, figures seen from the back play an equally important and suggestive role as those in frontal view; their opposition, a device which goes back to Italian Renaissance painting, is here used to diversify and balance the groups, as well as to enhance the timeless beauty of an everyday scene that is nevertheless sensed as charged with meaning.

BOYS PLAYING SOLDIERS
(Cat. No. 783)

The vigour and liveliness of the chief little soldier, his martial bearing, and the amusing, childish pride with which he faces the viewer mark this as one of the highest achievements in the portrayal of children to be found in the whole of Goya's oeuvre.

THE BALL GAME
(Cat. No. 784)

detail

Goya worked out this large composition to replace *The Blind Gui-tarist* as the centrepiece in the bedroom decoration.

Antechamber (1779-1780)

THE SWING
(Cat. No. 785)

The swing was frequently depicted in eighteenth-century painting, often, as in Boucher and Fragonard, with little-disguised erotic overtones. Goya here introduces it in what appears to be a peaceable family scene.

13

THE WASHERWOMEN
(Cat. No. 786)

The landscape in this work is one of the most naturalistic and beautiful in the whole series.

THE BULLFIGHT
(Cat. No. 787)

It has been suggested that the young bullfighter's features are those of Goya himself, who was a great fan of bullfighting.

THE TOBACCO GUARD
(Cat. No. 788)

Tobacco was a state monopoly in the eighteenth century, and since it was highly priced it was object of smugglers. Fetched high prices, and that illegal trade was a subject of topical interest and criticism in popular literature, where the law and its keepers are not rated for their efficiency.

THE WOODCUTTERS
(Cat. No. 791)
THE MAJO WITH A GUITAR
(Cat. No. 743)
THE RENDEZVOUS
(Cat. No. 792)

These cartoons evince a summary, shorthand technique, with energetic brushwork boldly and swiftly applied to the reddish underpainting with no attempt to cover it up.

The Decoration of the Dining Room of the Crown Prince in the Palace of El Pardo, 1786-1788

After a six-year hiatus, the Royal Tapestry Factory commissioned from Goya a new series, this time to furnish the dining room of the Crown prince in the palace of El Pardo. The cartoons were completed in the following year and the tapestries were woven; because of the death of Charles III, though, they were never hung in their original destination, but instead were randomly scattered in the Escorial royal residence. The theme chosen by Goya for the prince's private apartments was one that boasted a long iconographic tradition, the Four Seasons.

THE FLOWER GIRLS (SPRING)
(CAT. NO. 793)

A particularly lovely scene, pivoting on the elegance of the young woman who kneels in the foreground, in an echo of Velázquez's *Meninas*. She is offering a rose to the woman in the center, who is herself loaded with roses.

THE HARVEST (SUMMER)
(Cat. No. 794)

Goya has made here a lavish display of sheaves of wheat, the prime emblem of the goddess Ceres, who traditionally personified summer and the harvest in European painting. Country life is represented by the harvesters resting in the heat of summer: they are joined by their happy and smiling families in teasing a poor wretch whom they would like to get dead drunk.

15

The traditional iconography of the grape harvest is used here as an allegory of autumn. The airy, glowing landscape in which the gatherers are working reflects the tranquillity of the countryside and of nature as a whole. The smartly-dressed lady pensively reaches for the bunch of grapes proffered by a handsome *majo* attired in yellow, the colour of autumn, while the little boy, dressed up like a tiny prince, tries in vain to get his share of the savoury grapes, seemingly reserved for the grown-ups.

THE VINTAGE (AUTUMN)
(Cat. No. 795)

detail

THE SNOWSTORM
(WINTER)
(Cat. No. 798)

Winter is here signified by the blizzard and the snow-covered fields. Three peasants, wrapped in their blankets, return from an apparently unsuccessful trip to purchase a pig, since they proceed empty-handed, their dismal looks betraying cold and hunger. Two other men have had better luck: one covers himself with a hat and a warm cape, the other is dressed in livery, which possibly means that they are the servants of some nobleman. They are leading a mule, rather ornately harnessed and loaded with a huge pork cut down the middle.

THE WOUNDED MASON
(Cat. No. 796)

This is one of the most famous among Goya's tapestry cartoons, and it has been cited as proof of his concern for social issues, since it apparently shows a bricklayer injured on the job.

THE POOR AT THE FOUNTAIN
(Cat. No. 797)

The young mother, finely dressed with a shawl, red stockings and silver buckles on her black shoes, gazes tenderly and forbearingly at her youngest son while he bawls in a rage, perhaps because he has not been allowed to carry one of the jugs like his older brother.

Two Cats Fighting
(Cat. No. 6323)
A Magpie on a Tree Branch
(Cat. No. 7346)

These are cartoons for tapestries intended to hang over a doorway and in a corner, respectively. The cats pick up a frequent theme in Goya's oeuvre.

The Decoration of the Bedroom of the Infantas in the Palace of El Pardo, 1788-1789

In 1788 Goya was given a new commission, which he only completed in part: the cartoons for tapestries to decorate the bedroom of the Infantas, the daughters of Crown prince Carlos and his wife María Luisa. The death of king Charles III at the end of that year meant the abandonment of El Pardo, for the new royal pair preferred the palaces of La Granja, Aranjuez and El Escorial. The project is known from sketches preserved in the Museum.

Blindman's Buff
(Cat. No. 804)

Young persons dressed as *majos* and *majas* predominate in the merry circle, males alternating with females. It seems clear that the *majo* wielding a ladle in the center must have for his partner the young woman who in the preliminary sketch (Cat. No. 2781) is seen hiding behind the lady, apart from the ring. For some reason, Goya erased her out of the picture after having put her in.

The Decoration of the King's Office in El Escorial, 1791-1792

In April 1790 Goya was commissioned to furnish the cartoons for tapestries to be hung in the newly-crowned Charles IV's office within the royal apartments in the monastery of El Escorial. But at the end of 1792 he was taken with the illness that would leave him deaf, and after his recovery he did not go on with the commission. Charles IV had desired for his office "rustic and jolly subjects".

THE WEDDING
(Cat. No. 799)

This must count as one of the "jolly subjects" demanded by the king, although it reflects some of the deepest concerns of Goya the enlightened thinker. The lovely young woman in the centre, rather elaborately dressed up, has just been married to an obese, ugly man, obviously rich, whose profile resembles a pig's snout.

GIRLS AT THE FOUNTAIN (Cat. No. 800)

Both the girl in the foreground and the elder woman stare at the viewer with a knowing smile of complicity, as does their young escort; but only the girls precariously balance on their heads the water jugs, a traditional symbol of female virtue.

THE MANNEQUIN (Cat. No. 802)

The game of tossing a dummy in a blanket, a Carnival entertainment by its use of masks and mockery, becomes a clear Goyesque allegory of women's dominance over men.

PLAYING AT GIANTS (Cat. No. 800 a)
BOYS CLIMBING A TREE (CAT. No. 803)

In *Playing at Giants* the boys seem to mimic the game of the adult stiltwalkers, except that they ride piggyback on their playmates' shoulders.

PROFANE SUBJECTS, 1788-1828

The Drunken Mason

Blindman's Buff

The Hermitage of San Isidro on the Day of the Feast

The Meadow of San Isidro

Strolling Players

The Duchess of Alba and 'La Beata'

A Picador on Horseback

Witches in Flight

The Naked Maja

The Clothed Maja

Allegories of Commerce, Agriculture, and Industry

A Dead Turkey

Dead Fowl

The 2nd of May 1808 in Madrid. The Fight against the Mamelukes

The 3rd of May 1808 in Madrid: The Executions on Príncipe Pío Hill

The Colossus

The Milkmaid of Bordeaux

SKETCHES OF CARTOONS FOR THE BEDROOM OF THE INFANTAS IN THE PALACE OF EL PARDO AND FOR THE KING'S OFFICE IN EL ESCORIAL

The Prado Museum houses four of the most beautiful preliminary sketches for the cartoons of tapestries from the Santa Bárbara Royal Factory. They were purchased by the duke and duchess of Osuna in 1798, to be hung in La Alameda, their pleasure villa near Madrid, which already boasted other pictures by Goya. *The Drunken Mason* (Cat. No. 2782) is a model for the cartoon *The Wounded Mason* (Cat. No. 796). The modern title may be misleading, since, just as in the larger version, the man carried by his fellows is hurt: blood trickles from his left temple and down his shirt. The amused expression on his workmates' faces surely relates to the fact of his being in shirtsleeves, with no pants and one bare leg, which makes the traditional interpretation of the cartoon as a piece of social comment rather unlikely. The three sketches for the cartoons of tapestries to decorate the Infantas' bedroom in the Pardo Palace are without any doubt among the most significant and popular of Goya's works in the Prado. *Blindman's Buff* (Cat. No. 2781) epitomizes the lowbrow charm of Madrilenian *majos* and *majas*, a far cry from the idealized world of French rococo art. *The Hermitage of San Isidro on the Day of the Feast* (Cat. No. 2783) shows the hermitage of Madrid's patron saint on his feast day, the 15th of May. Young women dressed as *majas* are sitting on the ground in front of the chapel, waiting for their *majos* to bring them water to drink from the miraculous spring where a crowd lines up in the background. The theme is related to that of *The Meadow of San Isidro* (Cat. No. 750), the best-known piece in the series and also the most significant. Goya mentioned *The Meadow* in his letters to Martín Zapater, his child-

23

hood friend in Zaragoza, telling him of the difficulty of the task, with so many diverse groups of figures to cram into a small canvas. The composition is very precise, fully suggestive of the bustling festivity of the crowd sitting on the bank of the Manzanares River. The landscape opens up toward the river; beyond extends a topographically exact panorama of Madrid, where the bulky Royal Palace and Seminary are clearly visible, as well as the large dome of San Francisco el Grande and several easily recognized spires.

STROLLING PLAYERS
(Cat. No. 3045)

This picture, painted on tin, was part of a set of twelve scenes of bullfights and sundry subjects that the artist presented to the Academy of San Fernando in January 1794, after his serious illness the year before, which left him deaf. The handling is precise and very brilliant, with small and varied brush strokes, full of rhythm and movement, that stand out on the tin surface. On a makeshift stage above the sign "ALEC MEN", meaning 'Alegoría Menandrea', a satirical comedy is being played, in the style of those by the Greek Menander, a genre connected also with the Italian *Commedia dell'Arte*.

THE DUCHESS OF ALBA AND
'LA BEATA'
(Cat. No. 7020)

The mischievous, girlish character of the duchess is reflected in this small canvas signed "Goya Año 1795". Cayetana, in a yellow dress, with her back turned but identifiable by her lavish head of dark curly hair, is shown playing a prank on her chambermaid Rafaela Luisa Velázquez, nicknamed 'La Beata'.

A PICADOR ON HORSEBACK
(Cat. No. 744)

This was one of the pictures transferred from the Royal Palace to make up the initial core of the Prado collection, listed in its first catalogue (1821) as "Un picador a caballo". The very 'Goyesque' motif of a mounted bullfighter guarded the picture's secret until recent X-ray studies revealed an underlying equestrian portrait of Manuel Godoy.

Witches in Flight

This is one of a set of six small canvases with sorcery scenes that the duke and duchess of Osuna purchased from Goya in 1798, for their suburban villa near Madrid, La Alameda. Sorcery was a fashionable topic among aristocrats in the late eighteenth century; for the enlightened circles that Goya frequented, however, belief in witches was one of the evils of ignorance, a vulgar fraud, inimical to progress and reason.

The Naked Maja (Cat. No. 742)

This image, whose riddle has yet to be solved, is an exercise in confidential painting, a development of the cabinet picture tradition, and the 'capricho' *par excellence* in its depiction, at once traditional and

26

new, of the reclining female nude. This is no longer a classical Venus, perfect of body and face, escorted by Cupid; on the contrary, she is a living woman not exempt from blemishes, in spite of the undeniable allure and loveliness of her naked body. The painting was first recorded by Agustín Ceán Bermúdez and the engraver Pedro González de Sepúlveda, who in 1800 described it, fully installed and alone, without its clothed counterpart, in a private cabinet of Manuel Godoy's palace, along with other female nudes of classical stock, namely Velázquez's *Venus and Cupid* and a sixteenth-century Italian Venus, both of them gifts from the duchess of Alba to Godoy, and a copy of a Venus by Titian. Pictures of female nudity had been banned in Spain in the closing years of the eighteenth century, and both Charles III and Charles IV had considered destroying some works of that character in the royal collection; but apparently Godoy was accorded the exceptional privilege of keeping this kind of painting, albeit in the privacy of his rooms. A rumour starting very early in the nineteenth century had it that the model was the duchess of Alba, painted at the time of her affair with the artist in her estate of Sanlúcar de Barrameda, in 1796-1797. Others have suggested that she was Godoy's mistress Pepita Tudó, on the assumption that it was the queen's favourite who commissioned the work; in that case there would have been a still stronger reason to conceal the model's true face. By its outstanding expressive force, this painting has become a symbol of womanhood.

THE CLOTHED MAJA
(Cat. No. 741)

The Clothed Maja is first documented in an inventory made in 1808 by the French painter Frédéric Quilliet, José Bonaparte's agent, who lists it along with *The Naked Maja*. Both were mentioned again in 1813, as "Gitanas", gypsies, in the inventory made when Ferdinand VII seized the property of Godoy, and two years later they crop up in a report of the Secret Chamber of the Inquisition dated March 16, 1815, where one reads that "this Court hereby summons the aforesaid Goya to appear before it, to identify and declare whether they are his work, his motive for making them, commissioned by whom, and to what end". Once again, nothing is known about its commission, but the fact that it was not mentioned with its nude equivalent in 1800 might mean that it was done later, perhaps to dissimulate or cover the first.

ALLEGORIES
OF COMMERCE
(Cat. No. 2546),
AGRICULTURE
(Cat. No. 2547),
AND INDUSTRY
(Cat. No. 2548)

In late 1804 work was completed on the remodelling of Godoy's official residence in Madrid, which comprised building a vast hall of entrance and a grand staircase. Shortly afterwards, that magnificent entry was fitted with huge tondos that the prime minister had commissioned from Goya, to be painted in tempera with allegorical subjects. The allegories chosen were meant to portray the ideological foundations of wealth and progress in a new, enlightened Spain: Science (now lost), Agriculture, Industry and Commerce.

Profane Subjects

A DEAD TURKEY (Cat. No. 751)
DEAD FOWL
(Cat. No. 752)

These are two of a set of twelve still lifes belonging to Goya himself that were listed in an inventory of his property drawn up when his wife, Josefa Bayeu, died in 1812. He painted them as a decoration for his own home, surrounding himself with images that must have reminded him of his hunting feats. The sombre mood conveyed by the artist's insistence on the realistic rendering of dead animals has been taken as a sign that they were painted during the tragic years of the War of Independence.

The technical virtuosity of these two still lifes (the second signed "Goya") flawlessly reflects the distinctive quality of feathers as widely different as those of turkeys and hens.

THE 2ND OF MAY 1808 IN MADRID:
THE FIGHT AGAINST THE MAMELUKES (Cat. No. 748)

detail

The patriotism of Goya, who took up a resolute stance against the French invaders during the War of Independence, urged him to pay a tribute to the heroes of that struggle. Thus, when economic hardship struck him in the years following, he approached the regent, cardinal Luis de Borbón, with a proposal to celebrate some actions of the war in painting. His true feelings show through the catchphrases of rhetoric: "... to perpetuate by means of the brush the most notable and heroic actions and scenes of our glorious insurrection against the tyrant of Europe".

He was granted a monthly stipend of 1,500 *reales* to

execute four paintings, only two of which were completed. Their destination has never been precisely ascertained; it may have been a public monument to the Madrid heroes. Goya chose to illustrate two highly significant episodes, since it was the revolt of Madrilenians on May 2, 1808 that marked the beginning of the war, and the subsequent repression, with the shooting of prisoners, many of them innocent, reflected the cruelty of the war, the violence unleashed by the invasion, and the sufferings of the people, reduced to the role of a guiltless victim of events.

The scene of the 2nd of May shows the fierce, outraged onslaught of the commoners who, armed with knives and poniards, as true accounts testify, desperately attacked the mamelukes in the streets of Madrid, trying to prevent the departure of members of the royal family.

THE 3RD OF MAY 1808 IN MADRID:
THE EXECUTIONS ON PRÍNCIPE PÍO HILL
(Cat. No. 749)

The tragic events that followed on the people's uprising in Madrid on May 2, 1808 were well known to Spaniards. Literary descriptions and popular prints reported the French army's cruel repression of the people. Anyone the invaders caught bearing a knife —as craftsmen in Madrid usually did— was to be shot; and, according to Toreno, "they continued into the next morning, shooting some who had been arrested the day before, and they chose for the executions the fenced-in field of the house of

Príncipe Pío", in the Moncloa neighbourhood. The cheap prints minutely described the firing squads and their victims, but Goya has painted a scene that transcends the actual event to become a symbol of the innocence of victims, whose protagonism is absolute.

The night setting emphasizes the drama of the action, and the glare of the soldiers' lamp is focused on those who are about to die, some of them terrified at their inescapable fate, others furious but powerless. It also illuminates those who have already died, heaped in a bloody pile in the foreground; approaching from the dark distance may be seen some compassionate women, who combine with other details to confer on the scene the holy status of a sacrifice of innocents.

THE COLOSSUS
(Cat. No. 2785)

This painting has traditionally been identified with the one listed as "Un gigante", a giant, in the inventory of Goya's possessions drawn up in 1812, after the death of his wife. X-rays have revealed a totally different composition underneath, a blank, apparently unfinished landscape with the giant facing the viewer, his figure based on the Farnese Hercules, a classical sculpture that Goya copied more than once in his Italian Sketchbook.

THE MILKMAID OF BORDEAUX
(Cat. No. 2899)

This minor painting was inordinately praised by early twentieth-century Spanish critics who were eager to establish it as a necessary precedent of Impressionism.

RELIGIOUS PAINTINGS, 1775-1817

The Holy Family

Christ on the Cross

The Immaculate Conception

The Taking of Christ

Saints Justa and Rufina

THE HOLY FAMILY (Cat. No. 746)

No clue remains as to the original destination of this curious and lovely painting, which depicts one of the subjects most often repeated in Western art. The woman's features, her face a perfect classical oval, her lips brightly red and full, her dark flowing hair framing her countenance, are still reminiscent of those of the Virgin and her female companions in the frescoes of the Charterhouse of Aula Dei in Saragossa, painted by Goya in 1774.

CHRIST ON THE CROSS (Cat. No. 745)

With this painting, presented to the Royal Academy of Fine Arts of San Fernando in May 1780, Goya was finally admitted into that noble and progressive institution as an academician of merit, a status to which he had repeatedly aspired.

The figure of Christ, lit up against a very dark background, bears deeply devout echoes of seventeenth-century Spanish painting.

THE IMMACULATE CONCEPTION
(Cat. No. 3260)

A preliminary study for the main altarpiece, lost in the War of Independence, of the church of the College of Calatrava in Salamanca, a work recorded in 1783-1784 as a commission of Gaspar Melchor de Jovellanos (Cat. No. 3236), president of the Order of Calatrava, to whom this sketch belonged.

THE TAKING OF CHRIST
(Cat. No. 3113)

A sketch for an altarpiece in the sacristy of Toledo Cathedral, and one of the most interesting works by Goya because of its intrinsic and startlingly modern beauty, its swift, energetic and abstract brushwork defining the whole and the details with strict accuracy.

SAINTS JUSTA AND RUFINA
(Cat. No. 2650)

A friend of Goya, the scholar and collector Cean Bermúdez, asked him for a painting on this subject to hang in the sacristy of Seville Cathedral. This sketch on panel is the single remaining preliminary study, and it may have been also the last one, since it hardly differs from the final work. Goya travelled to Seville to examine the intended location and acquaint himself with other images of the city's patron saints. He kept to the traditional iconography of the two young martyrs, who are shown holding the palms of martyrdom and the clay vessels of their potter's trade; he also deferred to the local belief that they had protected the city during the earthquake of 1504, and so placed in the background the Cathedral and the Giralda tower, which, according to the pious sevillian legend, the two saints had miraculously held up.

PORTRAITS, 1783-1828

King Charles IV in Court Costume
Queen María Luisa in a Hooped Dress

Equestrian Portraits of King Charles IV and Queen María Luisa

The Family of Charles IV

Francisco de Paula
Carlos María Isidro
María Josefa
Antonio Pascual
Luis de Borbón

King Ferdinand VII in a Royal Mantle

María Teresa de Vallabriga

The Family of the Duke of Osuna

Doña María Antonia Gonzaga, Dowager Marchioness of Villafranca

The Marquis of Villafranca

The Painter Francisco Bayeu

Self-Portrait

Gaspar Melchor de Jovellanos

General Don José de Urrutia

María Tomasa de Palafox, Marchioness of Villafranca

Doña Joaquina Téllez-Girón y Pimentel, Marchioness of Santa Cruz

Juana Galarza de Goicoechea
Manuela Goicoechea y Galarza

The Actor Isidoro Máiquez

General Don José Palafox on Horseback

Self-Portrait

Manuela Téllez-Girón y Pimentel, Duchess of Abrantes

An Unknown Woman (Josefa Bayeu?)

Juan Bautista Muguiro

Royal Portraits

KING CHARLES IV IN COURT COSTUME (Cat. No. 3224)
QUEEN MARÍA LUISA IN A HOOPED DRESS (Cat. No. 2862)

In January 1789 Goya was commissioned to paint the first official portraits of the new monarchs after Charles III's demise. Both are portrayed full-length on large-format canvases, in court dress and wearing the insignia of royalty.

EQUESTRIAN PORTRAITS OF KING CHARLES IV AND QUEEN MARÍA LUISA (CAT. Nᵒˢ. 719 AND 720)

Along with *The Family of Charles IV* and *A Picador on Horseback*, these portraits were the only specimens of Goya's art that hung in the Prado Museum when it first opened in 1819, while the painter was still alive. Dated first is that of the queen, riding on *Marcial*, a gift from Godoy.

Goya modelled his equestrian portraits on those painted by Velázquez for the Salón de Reinos in the Buen Retiro Palace (now in the Prado), which he knew well, having made etched copies of them some years back.

THE FAMILY OF
CHARLES IV
(Cat. No.
726)

The grand family portrait of Charles IV is one of the main pillars of Goya's oeuvre and a sure guide to his style. It was painted in Aranjuez and Madrid during the spring and summer of 1800. There was a clear precedent in Spain for this kind of group portrait of royalty, a canvas where the French painter Van Loo had presented the family of Philip V, grandfather of Charles IV (Prado Museum, Cat. No. 2283). The fact that Goya may be seen at his easel on the left, like Velázquez in *Las meninas*, has prompted critics to stress unfailingly his indebtedness to that famous work, even though that is the only parallel to be found between both paintings, which in terms of subject, technique or composition are otherwise totally unrelated. Goya's picture is profoundly original, and his robust rendering stands as a symbol of the Bourbon monarchy and the protagonists of an era that came to an abrupt end with the invasion of Spain by Napoleon's troops and the War of Independence.

The centre of the stage is held by the frontal figure of the queen, her head turned slightly to the right with the smiling, attractive expression she wears in all her portraits. She is embracing her youngest daughter, the

Infanta María Isabel, and holding the hand of her youngest son, the Infante Francisco de Paula, who links her figure to that of the king. Charles is standing somewhat apart and nearer the picture plane, like his eldest son, who appears on the left, dressed in blue. By that means Goya symbolically sets off young Ferdinand as the prince of Asturias and heir to the throne, placing behind him the Infante Carlos María Isidro, second in the line of succession. Next to the Crown prince may be seen the aged face of the king's sister, the Infanta María Josefa, and an unidentified young woman. Standing on the right behind the king are his brother, the Infante Antonio Pascual, and, seen in profile, the queen of Portugal Carlota Joaquina, no longer in Spain at the time. Closing the composition on the right stand the prince and princess of Parma, María Luisa Josefina and Luis de Borbón, who later became king of Etruria; the princess holds in her arms their son, the Infante Carlos Luis.

SKETCHES FOR THE FAMILY OF CHARLES IV

FRANCISCO DE PAULA
(Cat. No. 730)
CARLOS MARÍA ISIDRO
(Cat. No. 731)
MARÍA JOSEFA
(Cat. No. 729)
ANTONIO PASCUAL
(Cat. No. 733)
LUIS DE BORBÓN
(Cat. No. 732)

The Prado Museum owns five of the ten preliminary sketches that are recorded for *The Family of Charles*

IV, executed by the painter in Aranjuez in June and July 1800. They share a more or less uniform size and an orange-reddish underpainting on which Goya summarily and quickly noted down the features of several of the king's relatives in half-length. He must have planned the composition painstakingly, and probably made several rough sketches of the whole.

KING FERDINAND VII IN A ROYAL MANTLE
(Cat. No. 735)

Ferdinand VII was born in El Escorial in 1784, the first son of Charles IV and María Luisa, and ascended the throne after the War of Independence. Goya certainly knew him well since childhood, but did not portray him until he was sixteen, in *The Family of Charles IV*. Now, in 1815, when he had abolished the Constitution and was reigning as an absolute monarch who repressed with needless cruelty any liberal move, Goya probably looked on him with small sympathy. The young king is here shown with all the insignia of royalty, in a crimson mantle lined with ermine and holding in his right hand the scepter with the arms of Castile and León; he wears the sash of

Charles III and the Golden Fleece.

Some pentimenti suggest that Goya elaborated as he went along, directly in front of the model; hence the astonishing mastery of the expression, with the vacuous smile belied by a suspicious glance.

Other Portraits and Self-Portraits

MARÍA TERESA DE VALLABRIGA
(Cat. No. 7695)

María Teresa de Vallabriga, the daughter of minor nobles in Aragón, was married in 1776 to don Luis de Borbón, brother of Charles III, who thereupon forfeited his and his descendants' rights to the throne. María Teresa, who was born in 1759, is seen here a few years after her marriage. The wooden base produces an enamel-like surface, while the dark, almost black underpainting highlights the terse and glowing whiteness of the youthful face. Profile portraits have a long tradition that goes back to the medals and coins of classical Antiquity.

THE FAMILY OF THE DUKE OF OSUNA
(Cat. No. 739)

This big canvas, for which Goya was paid 12,000 *reales*, is an exception in Spanish painting, scarcely given to this kind of family portrayal. Shown are the aristocrats doña Josefa Alonso de Pimentel, countess-duchess of Benavente, and don Pedro Téllez-Girón, the ninth duke of Osuna, who were among the earliest, most important and steadfast of Goya's patrons. The duke and duchess are accompanied by their children at that time: Josefa Manuela, the eldest, standing beside her father; Joaquina, later marchioness of Santa Cruz (Cat. No. 7070); little Francisco de Borja, the future duke of Osuna, playfully riding on a stick; and in the foreground, sitting on a cushion and holding the string of a toy carriage, the youngest son, Pedro de Alcántara, later prince of Anglona and future director of the Prado Museum during the liberal triennium, from 1821 to 1823.

The duke, dressed in uniform, was a soldier by training, a leading figure of the Enlightenment and a man of varied cultural and scientific interests. He presided over the Economic Society of Madrid and was a member of the Royal Spanish Academy. The duchess, a sensitive and cultured woman who patronized writers and artists, was president of the ladies' board within the Economic Society of Madrid. She is dressed according to French fashion, in a white crêpe gown adorned with rare and costly hand-painted buttons. The children are neatly attired in the kind of comfortable and loose-fitting clothes that children should wear according to the ideas of the Enlightenment

DOÑA MARÍA ANTONIA GONZAGA,
DOWAGER MARCHIONESS OF VILLAFRANCA (Cat. No. 2447)

Widowed in 1773 of don Antonio Álvarez de Toledo, the tenth marquis of Villafranca, she was the mother of don José Álvarez de Toledo (Cat. No. 2449), the eleventh marquis of Villafranca, and duke of Alba by his marriage. This intimate and sober image, exempt of the formalities and elaborate pomp of full-length portraits, shows her dressed with elegance and some coquetry in her adornment; she is holding a closed fan, and her attitude, rendered with realism, would seem to denote calm patience and authority.

THE MARQUIS OF VILLAFRANCA
(Cat. No. 2449)

Don José Alvarez de Toledo y Gonzaga, born an eldest son in 1756, inherited the title of duke of Villafranca on the death of his father in 1773. He married Cayetana, the duchess of Alba, in 1775, when he was nineteen and she thirteen. He died childless in 1796, the year after being portrayed by Goya. He was a man of artistic and musical tastes, and a counsellor of the Royal Academy; he reputedly played the violin like a virtuoso, he collected musical instruments, and the fact that he commissioned works directly from Haydn shows that he was in touch with the musical avant-garde.

The marquis is portrayed leaning his elbow on a fortepiano and gazing at the viewer as if to comment on the score, inscribed "Four Songs with Fortepiano Accompaniment, by Mr. Haydn". By his delicate features and hands and his refined pose, Goya conveys the sensitivity of the aristocrat and his love of music; but by presenting him in a smart riding suit complete with boots and spurs, his hat just put down on the piano, he is also suggesting, with his characteristic shrewdness, that the marquis wanted to have emphasized the virile interests that befit a nobleman.

THE PAINTER FRANCISCO BAYEU
(Cat. No. 721)

Bayeu was royal painter, director of the Academy of San Fernando and one of the leading figures in late eighteenth-century Spanish art. His portrait was commissioned from Goya by his daughter Feliciana Bayeu as a gift to the Academy in August 1795, upon the elder painter's death. It was delivered unfinished.

SELF-PORTRAIT

This small self-portrait belonged to the duchess of Alba, who bequeathed it to her butler Tomás de Berganza. It must have been a gift from the artist to that celebrated aristocrat at the time of their closest association, in 1795-1797, when Goya became intimate with Cayetana to the point of being her guest for some months at her estate in Sanlúcar de Barrameda.

GASPAR MELCHOR DE JOVELLANOS
(Cat. No. 3236)

was Minister of Justice. A prominent bronze statue of the goddess Minerva, set on a solid pedestal behind the politician's desk, seems to extend towards him a protecting hand, while leaning on a shield with the arms of the Royal Asturian Institute of Navigation and Mineralogy, which Jovellanos had founded.

An Asturian by birth, interested in the arts and sciences, Gaspar Melchor de Jovellanos played a leading role in the cultural and political life of Spain during the last third of the eighteenth century.

This portrait, signed "Jovellanos/por/Goya", is dated in 1798, when the sitter

His enlightened ideas are well known through his abundant and manifold writings on social and political issues, and from his position as a minister he tried to bring about significant reforms. Here he appears sitting on a carved and gilt armchair before a magnificent matching desk.

Goya has succeeded in capturing his serene, intelligent gaze; while placing him in a sumptuous setting, he shows him dressed with sober elegance, in an ermine-lined dress coat surprisingly devoid of the decorations, that were a usual adjunct of the images of public men.

GENERAL DON JOSÉ DE URRUTIA
(CAT. NO. 736)

Urrutia, born in 1739 in the Biscayan district of Zalla and deceased in 1809, attained to the honourable rank of captain-general by his own merits and valour on the battlefield. In 1789 he fought in the first Crimean war, and his conduct at the siege of Ozaku earned him the Cross of Saint George from the empress Catherine of Russia, who sent it along with a golden sword. In 1794 he was appointed captain-general of Catalonia, and confirmed the following year, after the Peace of Basel; but some time later he was discharged from all public duties owing to differences with Godoy. The handsome military bearing of the general, and the sweeping background landscape, relate to portraits by Reynolds and Raeburn, which Goya may have known through prints.

MARÍA TOMASA DE PALAFOX, MARCHIONESS OF VILLAFRANCA (Cat. No. 2448)

She was born in 1780, a daughter of the countess of Montijo, and married Francisco de Borja Álvarez de Toledo y Gonzaga, who upon the death of his brother, the eleventh marquis of Villafranca (Cat. No. 2449), came into the family title and joined it to that of Medina-Sidonia. María Tomasa, who came from an art-loving and cultured family, was herself an amateur painter and became an honorary member of the Academy of San Fernando. In this portrait, signed "*Goya 1805*" and exhibited at the Academy later in that year, she is shown painting her husband.

Doña Joaquina Téllez-Girón y Pimentel,
Marchioness of Santa Cruz (Cat. No. 7070)

Born in 1784, a daughter of the duke and duchess of Osuna, and made marchioness of Santa Cruz by her marriage to don José Gabriel de Silva y Waldstein in 1801, she was one of the most admired women of her time on account of her beauty and culture, a friend of poets and men of letters; Goya had portrayed her as a child with her family (Cat. No. 739).

Here she appears crowned with grapevine, her left arm resting on a lyre-shaped guitar that alludes to the classical god Apollo; thus Goya signals her fondness of poetry and her patronage of contemporary poets, presenting her, in the neoclassical vocabulary of the time, as a modern Erato, the muse of lyric poetry. By its excellent condition, this picture is exceptional in maintaining its original appearance, with tonal harmonies of a dazzling perfection.

JUANA GALARZA DE GOICOECHEA
(Cat. No. 4194)
MANUELA GOICOECHEA Y
GALARZA (Cat. No. 7461)

On the occasion of his son Javier's marriage to Gumersinda Goicoechea in 1805, Goya painted six delightful miniature portraits of the bride's family: her father Miguel Martín de Goicoechea and her mother Juana Galarza, wealthy and liberal Madrid merchants who were the owners of a flourishing business of textiles and lace, and their four daughters. The Prado houses those of the mother and the eldest daughter, Manuela.

THE ACTOR ISIDORO MÁIQUEZ
(Cat. No. 734)

Born in Cartagena in 1768, of actor parents, Máiquez studied in Paris under Talma and imported into Spain his new and forceful acting style. This portrait, signed "Mayquez/Por Goya/1807", is dated the year before the War of Independence, and in it Goya's dramatic technique amazingly anticipates the future, even though it was probably calculated to meet such a specific condition as that of ensuring visibility from a distance without thereby lessening the force of the image.

GENERAL DON JOSÉ PALAFOX ON HORSEBACK
(CAT. NO. 725)

Palafox, a Saragossan born in 1775 and a popular hero in the War of Independence, was appointed captain-gen- eral of Saragossa in 1808. His skill as a politician and his gallantry as a soldier earned him the favour of both the

Cortes and the people. He turned his home city into a symbol of patriotic resistance against the invaders, even at the cost of countless lives. This portrait, inscribed "El Excmo. Sr. D. José Palafox y Melci, por Goya, año de 1814", was one that the painter felt especially satisfied with. It shows the horse rushing ahead, and the general, who wears in his hat the badge of the defenders of Saragossa, raising his sword as a signal to attack. The dark hues of the broad and bare landscape enhance the glowing image of the hero in a brightly lit foreground.

SELF-PORTRAIT
(Cat. No. 723)

Signed "Fr. Goya Pintor [?] Aragonés/Por el mismo/1815". This outstandingly individual and intimate likeness was perhaps painted by the artist for his own home and the people nearest to him in the grim aftermath of the war against Napoleon, while political persecution under Ferdinand VII grew steadily worse. Goya was soon to withdraw from public life and isolate himself within the circle of his family and his closest friends.

MANUELA TÉLLEZ-GIRÓN Y
PIMENTEL, DUCHESS OF ABRANTES

The sitter was a daughter of
the ninth duke of Osuna, born
in 1793 and married to Angel
María de Carvajal, the eighth
duke of Abrantes. She
received a modern education
and was fond of the arts and
letters. Her grandfather the
duke of Huesca inspired her
with a passion for music, and
it was as a singer that Goya
portrayed her in this canvas,
a commission from the
duchess of Osuna in 1816.
Inscribed "Doña Manuela
Girón y Pimentel. Duq.sa de Abrantes. Pr Goya/1816", this
is his last great likeness of a
highborn lady.

AN UNKNOWN WOMAN (JOSE-
FA BAYEU?)
(Cat. No. 722)

Tradition has it that this is
a portrait of Josefa Bayeu,
Goya's wife. However, the
date of execution, which
judging from the style of
clothing must be later than
1800, is not consistent with
the age of the purported
sitter, since Josefa Bayeu
died at sixty-five in 1812.

Juan Bautista Muguiro
(Cat. No. 2898)

Goya died in April 1828, and this is possibly his last known painting. The inscription mentioning his age, "D.n Juan de Muguiro, por/su amigo Goya, á los/81 años, en Burdeos,/Mayo de 1827", is an old man's proud assertion of his ability to rise above his infirmities; but it also carries a hint that he was not fit to paint much else in what was to prove the last year of his life. Contemporary references indicate that his failing eyesight compelled him to paint with a magnifying glass, and that he concentrated more on his drawings, lithographs and miniature paintings on ivory than on the larger canvases, which required more effort. The sure touch of his brush, which lasted him from youth to early old age, has now turned shaky or wavering. But that which in others might be a fault is here transformed, by the pictorial intelligence of the old master and his time-tried skill, into an abstract sublimation of matter, which is suggested with next to no support. Their sparkling, intangible colour suffices to recreate the papers and inkstand; for the wooden back of the chair or the yellow upholstery of its seat, Goya is satisfied with a few dashing strokes of his brush, without attempting to define form or material in the traditional way.

55

WALL PAINTINGS FROM THE QUINTA DEL SORDO ('BLACK PAINTINGS') (1820-1823)

The paintings that decorated the house bought in 1819 by Goya in the outskirts of Madrid, referred to as the Quinta del Sordo (House of the Deaf Man) before that date, have become popularly known by the name of 'Black Paintings' on account of the dark and black pigments used in them, and also because of their grim subject matter: witches and their sabbaths, the violence of Saturn devouring his children or of Judith beheading Holofernes.

Photographs taken in the nineteenth century show that Goya's new house was two-storied and quite commodious, and those characteristics must have been crucial for his decision to decorate it in his own way, using a medium such as mural painting, which he perfectly mastered and which made it possible for him to cover large wall expanses without too much exertion.

The painted decoration of the Quinta must have been executed between 1820, when Goya moved in, and 1823, when he left for Bordeaux. In 1828 his friend the painter Antonio Brugada, in whose arms Goya had died, made a full inventory of the house, including the 'Black

Paintings'. These were distributed in two rooms, one in the ground floor and the other, of similar size, upstairs; Brugada gave them titles that perhaps reflected the ideas of Goya himself.

The 'Black Paintings' remained in the Quinta, which the painter's grandson Mariano sold in 1859, until 1874. In 1873 the estate was acquired by baron Émile d'Erlanger, who, being interested only in the paintings, had them removed by the painter and restorer Salvador Martínez Cubells. The baron tried to sell them in Paris in 1878, with no success, and finally donated them to the Spanish state in 1883, whereupon they were assigned to the Prado Museum.

Their condition is less than satisfactory. The intervention of Martínez Cubells, although it may have saved them from destruction, probably did serious damage, since X-rays show extensive areas where the original colour was lost. They also reveal overpainting, retouching and modifications that intensify the sombre and dark mood of the scenes, more to the aesthetic taste of 1870, the date when they were restored, than to that of the period when Goya painted them.

The 'Black Paintings' have been crucial to the assessment of Goya's art in the modern world. The German expressionists, the surrealists and the representatives of other contemporary art movements, as well as writers and even filmmakers, have pointed to this series of compositions by the elderly Goya, who was by then cut off from the surrounding world and creating with absolute freedom, as the germ of modern art. In spite of the myriad explanations offered by art and literary historians, writers, and even psychologists, these works remain elusive and puzzling, not only because of the difficulty of unraveling their contents, but also on account of their staggering formal break with the art of their time and their thrust into the future; yet it is a fact that they display many of the aesthetic problems, moral concerns and forms of humour that preoccupied Goya since his youth. Connections may be discovered even with some drawings in the early Italian Sketchbook, or, somewhat later, with the figures in early tapestry cartoons like *The Blind Guitarist*.

The world of sorcery suited Goya to denounce the depravity of humans, whose very faces turn into beastly masks in the evillest 'witches', while the superstition and ignorance of the masses materialize in those pilgrimages and processions where individuals dress in the outworn fashion of the seventeenth century. War and the political events of the day have also a place, along with fratricidal and pointless violence, so that it may be said that these works do not stray far from the guiding lines of morality, rule of reason and progress that Goya advocated throughout his life by the vehicle of his art.

Other paintings by Goya not in the Prado Museum

Amsterdam: *Ramón Satué* (1823; Rijksmuseum).
Besançon: *Cannibals* (Musée).
Bilbao: *Leandro Fernández de Moratín* (ca. 1808; Museo de Bellas Artes).
Budapest: *The Knifegrinder* and *The Water Carrier* (ca. 1810; Museum).
Cádiz: *The Multiplication of Loaves and Fishes*, *The Last Supper* and *The Parable of the Wedding Garment* (1796-97; Oratorio de la Santa Cueva).
Cudillero (Asturias): *Hannibal Looking on Italy from the Alps* (1772; Fundación Selgas-Fagalde).
Chicago: *The Story of the Bandit Maragato* (1806-07; Art Institute).
Dallas: *The Madhouse* (1794; Meadows Museum).
London:
NATIONAL GALLERY: *The Picnic* (1788; sketch), *Witchcraft Scene* (1798), *Andrés del Peral* (ca. 1797).
WELLINGTON MUSEUM: *Wellington on Horseback* (1812).
Los Angeles: *Saint Jerome* (Norton Simon Museum).
Madrid:
ACADEMY OF SAN FERNANDO: *Self-Portrait at the Easel* (ca. 1790), *La Tirana*, *Manuel Godoy*, *Juan de Villanueva* (1800-05), *Ferdinand VII on Horseback* (1808), *An Inquisition Scene* (ca. 1810), *A Procession* (ca. 1810), *A Bullfight in a Village* (ca. 1810), *A Madhouse Scene* (ca. 1810).
BANCO DE ESPAÑA: *The Count of Floridablanca* (ca. 1783), *The Count of Altamira* (1787), *The Marquis of Tolosa* (1787), *Francisco Javier de Larrumbe* (1787), *The Count of Cabarrús* (1788).
CASA DUCAL DE ALBA: *The Duchess of Alba in White* (1795).
MUSEO LÁZARO GALDIANO: *The Witches' Sabbath*, *The Evil Spell* (1798), *The Harvest* (sketch), *The Entombment of Christ* (ca. 1780).
MUSEO MUNICIPAL: *Allegory of the City of Madrid* (1810).
CONVENTO DE LOS PADRES ESCOLAPIOS: *The Last Communion of Saint Joseph of Calasanz* (1819).
MUSEO ROMÁNTICO: *Saint Gregory the Great* (1796-98).
MUSEO THYSSEN-BORNEMISZA: *Asensio Juliá* (ca. 1798).
PALACIO REAL: *King Charles IV*, *Queen María Luisa*.
PALACIO DE LA ZARZUELA: *Making Bullets* (ca. 1810), *Making Gunpowder* (ca. 1810).
SAN ANTONIO DE LA FLORIDA: Frescoes with a miracle of Saint Anthony of Padua (1798).
SAN FRANCISCO EL GRANDE: *Saint Bernardino of Siena Preaching* (1782-83).
PRIVATE COLLECTIONS: *The Countess-Duchess of Benavente* (1785), *The Countess of Chinchón* (1799), *Ceán Bermúdez* (1798), *La Tirana*, *The Count and Countess of Fernán-Núñez* (1803), *Martín Miguel de Goicoechea* and *Juana Galarza* (1810), *A Shipwreck* (1794), *A Fire By Night* (1794), a series of scenes known as 'The Mar-

quis of La Romana paintings[1], *The Maja and the Celestina on the Balcony* (ca. 1812).

Málaga: *Mariano Goya* (1809; Collection Marqués de Larios).

Malibu (Los Angeles): *The Marchioness of Santiago* (1809; Paul Getty Museum).

Minneapolis: *Self-Portrait with Doctor Arrieta* (1820; Institute of Art).

New York:

METROPOLITAN MUSEUM: *The Countess of Altamira and Her Son* (1787-88), *Manuel Osorio y Zúñiga* (1788), *Tiburcio Pérez Cuervo* (1820).

FRICK COLLECTION: *María Martínez de Puga* (1824).

HISPANIC SOCIETY: *The Duchess of Alba in Black*.

PRIVATE COLLECTION: *Still Life with Dead Hares* (ca. 1800).

Pamplona: *The Marquis of San Adrián* (1804; Museo de Bellas Artes, Diputación Foral).

Paris:

MUSÉE DU LOUVRE: *The Marchioness of La Solana* (ca. 1795), *Ferdinand Guillemardet* (1798).

PRIVATE COLLECTION: Portraits of *Javier Goya in Grey and of His Wife* (1806).

Corte di Mamiano (Reggio Emilia): *The Family of the Infante Don Luis* (1783; Fondazione Magnani-Rocca).

Rome:: Portraits of *Joaquín María Ferrer and of His Wife* (1824; private collection).

Saragossa:

MUSEO: *The Virgin of El Pilar, The Death of Saint Francis Xavier* (ca. 1772).

BASÍLICA DEL PILAR: Frescoes in the Coreto, *The Adoration of the Name of God* (1775); Dome, *The Queen of Martyrs* (1780).

CARTUJA DE AULA DEI: Frescoes with the Life of the Virgin (1774).

IBERCAJA: *Self-portrait* (1778)

Seville:

CATHEDRAL: *Saints Justa and Rufina* (1814).

PRIVATE COLLECTION: *The Annunciation* (1785).

Stockholm: *Allegory of Time, Truth and History* (ca. 1798; Nationalmuseum).

Switzerland: *Majas on the Balcony* (ca. 1812; private collection).

Toledo: *The Taking of Christ* (1798; Cathedral, Sacristy).

Valencia:

CATHEDRAL: *Saint Francis Borgia and a Possessed Man, Saint Francis Borgia Taking Leave of His Family* (1788).

MUSEO: *Joaquina Candado*.

Valladolid: *The Death of Saint Joseph, Saint Lutgard, Saints Bernard and Robert* (1787; Convento de Santa Ana).

Washington: *The Marchioness of Pontejos* (ca. 1786), Portraits of *Bartolomé Sureda and of His Wife* (ca. 1804-06), *Francisca Sabasa y García* (ca. 1804-08), *The Bookseller's Wife* (ca. 1808).

Chronology

1746 Goya is born on March 30 in Fuendetodos (Saragossa).

1759 Studies painting and drawing in Saragossa, in the workshop of José Luzán.

1763 First trip to Madrid.

1766 Second trip to Madrid.

1771 Travels in Italy, with a lengthy stay in Rome. He also visits Venice, Parma, Genoa and other cities. Enters competition at the Academy of Parma.

1773 Marries Joseta Bayeu, sister of Francisco and Ramón.

1774 Frescoes in the Charterhouse of Aula Dei in Saragossa.

1775 Fresco on a vault of the Basílica del Pilar in Saragossa.

1776 First commissions of tapestry cartoons for the king, a kind of work he will paint until 1792.

1780 Elected academician of merit to the Royal Academy of Fine Arts of San Fernando.

1783 Works for the Infante don Luis de Borbón, brother of the king.

1785 Appointed assistant director of painting at the Academy.

1786 Appointed King's Painter. Birth of Javier, the only son that will survive him.

1790 Last series of tapestries for the royal palaces.

1792 Visits Cádiz and Seville, where he is taken seriously ill.

1793 Convalesces in Andalusia but is left deaf. Returns to Madrid in the summer.

1794 Presents to the Academy twelve cabinet pictures that mark the beginning of his independent production.

1795 Appointed director of painting at the Academy.

1796 Stays in Seville with Ceán Bermúdez. Relationship with the duchess of Alba begun in Sanlúcar de Barrameda.

1797 Second stay with the duchess of Alba in Sanlúcar. Resigns his directorship of painting at the Academy.

1798 Frescoes in the hermitage of San Antonio de la Florida.

1799 Etchings series, *Los Caprichos*. Appointed First King's Painter.

1804 Gregorio Ferro, a thoroughly neoclassical painter, obtains general directorship of the Academy against Goya.

1805 Javier Goya marries. Goya meets Leocadia Zorrilla.

1806 Birth of his grandson Mariano.

1808 Goya, an official at court, takes an oath of loyalty to king José Bonaparte.

1810 Draws his will with his wife Josefa Bayeu.

1811 José Bonaparte awards him the Royal Order of Spain.

1812 Death of Josefa Bayeu.

1814 Is cleared of charges of collaborating with the government of José Bonaparte. Attends a solemn session of the Academy presided by Ferdinand VII.

1816 Etchings series, *La Tauromaquia*. Begins *Los Disparates*.

1819 Tries lithography, a new technique. Falls gravely ill. Buys the 'Quinta del Sordo', a estate outside Madrid. Lives with Leocadia Zorrilla and her daughter Rosarito, possibly his as well.

1820 Attends his last session at the Academy. Swears loyalty to the king and the Constitution.

1824 Asks leave from the king to take a water cure at Plombières in France. Goes to Paris in June, and to Bordeaux in September; Leocadia and Rosarito join him.

1825 Is extremely ill. Lithographs, *The Bulls of Bordeaux*. Miniatures on ivory.

1826 In Madrid, petitions the king for retirement; is granted a pension of 50,000 *reales*.

1827 Again in Madrid; returns to Bordeaux in September.

1828 Dies in Bordeaux on April 16, in his last home, rue Fossés-de-l'Intendance.

Selected Bibliography

ÁGUEDA, Mercedes, "Los retratos ecuestres de Goya", in *Goya. Nuevas visiones. Homenaje a Enrique Lafuente Ferrari*, Madrid, 1987, pp. 39-59.

ANDIOC, René, "En torno a los cuadros del Dos de Mayo en Goya", Osnabrück University, 1991.

ANGULO ÍÑIGUEZ, Diego, "El *Saturno* y las Pinturas Negras de Goya", *Archivo Español de Arte*, 1962, pp. 173-77.

ARNAIZ, José Manuel, *Francisco de Goya. Cartones y tapices*, Madrid, 1987.

BEROQUI, Pedro, "Una biografía de Goya escrita por su hijo", *Archivo Español de Arte*, 1927, pp. 99-100.

BERUETE, Aureliano de, *Goya, pintor de retratos*, Madrid, 1916.

BERUETE, Aureliano de, *Goya, composiciones y figuras*, Madrid, 1917.

BOZAL, Valeriano, *Imagen de Goya*, Madrid, 1983.

CAMÓN AZNAR, José, *Francisco de Goya*, 4 vols., Zaragoza, 1980-82.

CRUZADA VILLAAMIL, G., *Los tapices de Goya*, Madrid, 1870.

GÁLLEGO, Julián, *Las "Majas" de Goya*, Madrid, 1982.

GARRIDO, Carmen, "Algunas consideraciones sobre la técnica de las Pinturas Negras de Goya", *Boletín del Museo del Prado*, 1984, pp. 4-40.

GASSIER, P., and WILSON, J., *Vie et Oeuvre de Francisco de Goya*, Freiburg, 1970.

GLENDINNING, N., *The Interpretation of Goya's Black Paintings*, London, 1977.

GUDIOL, José, *Goya 1746-1828: Biografía, estudio analítico y catálogo de sus pinturas*, 4 vols., Barcelona, 1970.

HELD, Jutta, *Die Genrebilder der Madrider Teppichmanufaktur und die Anfänge Goyas*, Berlin, 1971.

HELMAN, Edith, *Trasmundo de Goya*, Madrid, 1983.

LAFUENTE FERRARI, E., *Antecedentes, coincidencias e influencias del arte de Goya*, Madrid, 1947 (ed. 1987).

LICHT, Fred, *Goya, The Origins of the Modern Temper in Art*, London, 1979.

LUNA, J., and MORENO, M., *Goya. 250 Aniversario*, Madrid, Museo del Prado, 1996.

MENA, M., and URREA, J., *El Cuaderno italiano de Goya*, Madrid, Museo del Prado, 1994

MULLER, Priscilla, *Goya's Black Paintings. Truth and Reason in Light and Liberty*, New York, 1984.

PÉREZ SÁNCHEZ, A. E., "Goya en el Prado. Historia de una colección singular", in *Goya. Nuevas visiones, Homenaje a Enrique Lafuente Ferrari*, Madrid, 1987, pp. 307-22.

PITA ANDRADE, J. M., "Observaciones en torno a los cartones para tapices", *Goya*, 1979, pp. 232-59.

PITA ANDRADE, J. M., *Goya. Obra, vida y sueños*, Madrid, 1989.

ROSE, Isadora, *Manuel Godoy, patrón de las artes y coleccionista*, 2 vols., Madrid, 1983.

SALAS, Xavier de, "Un boceto de Goya para la Inmaculada del Colegio de Calatrava", *Archivo Español de Arte*, 1977, pp. 1-8.

SALAS, Xavier de, "Minucias sobre Goya. Sobre el significado de las Pinturas Negras de la Quinta", *Estudios sobre literatura y arte dedicados al Prof. Emilio Orozco Díaz*, Granada, 1979, pp. 245-58.

SALAS, Xavier de, *Goya en Madrid*, Madrid, 1979.

SAMBRICIO, V. de, *Tapices de Goya*, Madrid, 1946.

SÁNCHEZ CANTÓN, F. J., "Goya, pintor religioso", *Revista de Ideas Estéticas*, 1946, pp. 277-310.

SÁNCHEZ CANTÓN, F. J., *Vida y obras de Goya*, Madrid, 1951.

SÁNCHEZ CANTÓN, F. J., *Goya y sus Pinturas Negras de la Quinta del Sordo*, Madrid, 1963.

TOMLINSON, Janice, *Goya. The Tapestry Cartoons and Early Career at the Court of Madrid*, New York, 1989.

TORRECILLAS, Carmen, "Nueva documentación fotográfica sobre las pinturas de la Quinta del Sordo de Goya", *Boletín del Museo del Prado*, 1985, pp. 87-99.

VIÑAZA, Conde de la, *Goya. Su tiempo, su vida, sus obras*, Madrid, 1887.

WILSON-BAREAU, J., *Goya. El Capricho y la Invención. Cuadros de gabinete, bocetos y miniaturas*, Madrid, Museo del Prado, 1993 (Eng. ed. 1994).

YRIARTE, Charles, *Goya. Sa biographie, les fresques, les toiles, les tapisseries, les eaux-fortes et le catalogue de l'oeuvre*, Paris, 1867.

63

General Information on the Prado Museum

EDIFICIO VILLANUEVA
Paseo del Prado, s/n
28014 Madrid
Telephone:
91 330.28.00
Fax:
91 330.28.56
Information:
91 330.29.00
Wheelchair access available

VISITING HOURS
Tuesday through Saturday:
9:00 a.m. to 7:00 p.m.
Sundays and holidays:
9:00 a.m. to 2:00 p.m.
Closed on *Mondays*

ENTRANCE FEES
General Admission   *500 ptas*

Spanish youth card, student card, or international equivalents.
Cultural and education group rates (by advance request)
91 330.28.25)   *250 ptas*

Senior citizens over 65 or pensioners.
Members of the Fundación Amigos del Museo del Prado.
Cultural and educational volunteers   *Free*

Free General Admission Days
Saturdays, from 2:30 p.m. to 7:00 p.m.
Sundays, from 9:00 a.m. to 2:00 p.m.

Coffee Shop
Tuesday to Saturday:
9:30 a.m. to 6:30 p.m
Sundays and holidays:
9:30 a.m. to 1:30 p.m.

Restaurant
Monday to Saturday:
9:30 a.m. to 6:30 p.m.

Shops
Tuesday to Saturday:
9:30 a.m. to 6:30 p.m.
Sundays and holidays:
9:30 a.m. to 1:30 p.m.

HOW TO GET THERE
Metro:
Atocha, Banco and Retiro stations

Bus:
Numbers 9, 10, 14, 19, 27, 34, 37, 45

From the airport:
Airport shuttle bus to Plaza de Colón, then No. 27 bus

General Information about the Fundación Amigos del Museo del Prado
Museo del Prado
c/ Ruiz de Alarcón,nº 21 – bajo. 28014 Madrid
Tel: 91 420.20.46
Fax.: 91 429.50.20
E-mail: famprado@canaldata.es

Office hours:
Monday to Friday, from 9:30 a.m. to 2:30 p.m.